Bookshelf

PUZZLERS

LEVEL FOUR

Alison and Graham White

Oliver & Boyd

Contents

Introduction for Pupils

Read the story *The Silver Sword* either to yourself or with your teacher. Before you start, read the introduction and look at the picture. You will find that there are twelve words missing from the story. Do not stop reading when you come to a space but read past it trying to make sense of the story. Do the same when you come to the second space. Try to read to the end of the story to work out what is happening.

Go back to the start of the story and when you come to the first space, look at No. 1 on the list of words that will fit the spaces. You will see that there are four words – *properly, completely, warmly, herself.* Each of these words can fit into the story and make sense. You may have thought of one of these words or you may have thought of another word that still sounds right. Any word is correct as long as it makes sense and sounds right.

Now look at space No. 2 and look at No. 2 on the list of words that will fit the spaces. Again there are four words and again each word can fit into the story and make sense. You may have thought of another word which also sounds right.

Do the same thing with the other spaces.

As you can see, any word you choose makes sense. One word may alter the story slightly but it still makes sense. Remember also that one word is not the correct or best answer, any of the words will do.

In any space there may be more than four words which have been thought about by other children, and they may all still sound right and make sense. There are twelve other stories in this book and you will be asked to do the same thing as you have done in this story. The only difference will be that you will not have a list of words to choose from; you will have to think of the words that make sense. Once you have thought about the words, your teacher will discuss them with you.

All the stories in this book come from longer stories which you might like to read. All the stories are published by Puffin.

Demonstration Unit: Level Four

The Silver Sword

by Ian Serraillier

During the Second World War the Germans invaded Poland. Warsaw, the capital, was run by the Nazis and everyone was terrified of them. One night they arrived at the Balicki's house and took away both parents. Edek, their son, fired his gun at the Nazis, who then locked the three children in the house.

'We must get away from here before they come back,' said Ruth.

With some difficulty she dressed Bronia, while Edek went into the hall to fetch overcoats and boots and fur caps.

There was no time for Ruth to dress _ _1_ _ . She put on a coat over her nightdress and wound a woollen scarf round Bronia.

'We can't get out the front way,' said Edek. 'There's another van coming. I heard the whistle.'

'What about the back?' said Ruth.

'The wall's too high. We'd never get Bronia over. Besides, there are Nazis _ _2_ _ in that street. There's only one way – over the roof.'

'We'll never manage that,' said Ruth.

'It's the only way,' said Edek. 'I'll carry Bronia. Be quick – I can hear them coming.'

He picked up the _ _3_ _ Bronia and led the way upstairs. He was wearing his father's thick overcoat over his pyjamas, a pair of stout boots on his bare feet, and his rifle slung on his back.

When they were all up in the attic, he _ _4_ _ the skylight.

'Now listen, Bronia,' said Edek. 'If you make a _ _5_ _ , we shall never see Mother again. We shall all be killed.'

'Of course we shall see her again,' Ruth added. 'But only if you do as Edek says.'

He climbed through the skylight on to the _ _6_ _ roof. Ruth handed Bronia up to him, then followed herself. The bitterly cold air made her gasp.

'I can't carry you yet, Bronia,' said Edek. 'You must walk behind me and hold on to the rifle. It doesn't matter if you _ _7_ _ , if you hold on to the rifle. And don't look down.'

The first few steps – as far as the V between the chimney and the roof ridge – were _ _8_ _ . Edek made a dash for it, grabbed the telephone bracket and hauled himself up, with Bronia clinging on behind. She was speechless with terror. He reached back and hauled Ruth up after him.

After a few moments' rest, they slid down a few feet on to a flat part that jutted out, a sort of parapet.

The roof ridge lay between them and the street, so they could not see what was happening down there. _ _9_ _ they could hear shouting, the whine of cars, the screech of brakes.

Luckily for them, all the houses on this side of the school were joined together in one long terrace, otherwise they could not have got away. Even so, it was a miracle that none of their slips and tumbles ended in _ _10_ _ .

They must have gone fully a hundred yards when the first explosion shook the air. A sheet of fire leapt up from their home into the frosty night sky. They fell flat in the snow and lay there. The _ _11_ _ shook, the whole city seemed to tremble. Another

explosion. Smoke and flames poured from the windows. Sparks showered into the darkness.

'Come along,' said Edek. 'We shan't let them have us now.'

With growing confidence they hurried along the roof-tops. At last, by descending a twisted fire escape, they reached street level. On and on they hurried, not knowing or caring where they went so long as they left those _ 12 _ flames behind them.

They did not stop till the fire was far away and the pale winter dawn was breaking.

They took shelter in the cellar of a bombed house. Exhausted, huddled together for warmth, they slept till long after midday, when cold and hunger woke them.

Possible Words

  1. properly, completely, warmly, herself.
  2. billeted, stationed, living, patrolling.
  3. sobbing, crying, terrified, frightened.
  4. smashed, broke, opened, lifted.
  5. sound, noise, fuss, squeak.
  6. slippery, sloping, tiled, steep.
  7. slip, slide, fall, slither.
  8. ghastly, dreadful, difficult, awful.
  9. But, However, Nevertheless, Still.
10. disaster, tragedy, catastrophe, trouble.
11. roof, building, chimney, house.
12. roaring, blazing, furious, horrible.

1 The Bongleweed

by Helen Cresswell

Within a few days of Becky and Jason planting the seeds, the Bongle-weed had completely covered the churchyard beside Becky's garden. It turned into an enormous plant with huge but glorious flowers and still continued to grow!

It was *there*, still out there in the dark at this very moment, breathing and growing, while the coffee cups clattered and the curtains were drawn and nothing would ever be the same again.

She tried, for the first time, to dare to imagine how it would all end.

'If it actually grew and grew and grew and grew,' she thought. 'Then what?'

The idea was beyond words, so she tried to see it in pictures, and first of all she saw the Bongleweed up on the _ _1_ _ of their own house, thatching it green and putting flower flames on the chimney pots, shuttering the windows, roping the doors. (Or even coming *in* through the door, if it happened to be open – she almost squealed _ _2_ _ at the thought – climbing over chairs and tables and up the stairs while Else did _ _3_ _ battle with broom and kitchen knife.)

Once she had formed a clear picture of _ _4_ _ , it was an easy step to see the whole village cocooned, the _ _5_ _ shut out and the people chopping narrow lanes through the jungle, tunnels from house to house so that they could go and _ _6_ _ in one another's greenish-lit kitchens and wonder where it would all end, and _ _7_ _ the fire brigade would arrive and get them out.

'I suppose it *would* be the fire brigade's job,' she thought. 'Like if you get your head stuck in the _ _8_ _ railings. You dial 999 and they send the fire brigade.'

But the telephone wires? Surely the Bongleweed would run _ _9_ _ them at the speed of light, throwing out those thick branches and cucumbery leaves until they _ _10_ _ under the sheer weight of greenery? The Bongleweed went north, south, east, west and skyward – it would make for Brum to the north and London to the south. The _ _11_ _ way, she knew, would be the M1, and she could see it, quite _ _12_ _ , the long green length of the motorway, silent now, with warning lights flashing non-stop somewhere deep under, and now and again the plaintive, muffled hooting of a trapped motorist . . .

2 The Almost All~White Rabbity Cat

by Meindert De Jong

Rosita, the cat, found Barney all alone in the flat when she slid her paws under the locked front door and opened it! He loved her and wanted to keep her but when she disappeared he persuaded his mother to help him search the block of flats. They decided to start on the top floor.

On the elevator Barney became sober. 'Mother,' he said, 'if Rosita went into an apartment with nobody there but a dog . . .'

'You do have the nicest ideas!' Mother laughed at him. 'Why don't you think big if you want to scare yourself, why not an alligator or a _ _1_ _ ?'

Barney laughed doubtfully and shivered a little. Mother sure was feeling wild on her free afternoon. *He* was worried.

'Look,' Mother told him, 'if we knock and nobody comes, I'll make rickety-tickety _ _2_ _ on the door and if Rosita is inside

she'll surely come to the door and I can wriggle my fingers
_ _3_ _ it and if a white paw shoots out, well, there's your Rosita.
Then we can open the door. Okay?'

'But _ _4_ _ out for a biting dog,' Barney warned. 'Don't stick
your fingers through too far – you're just learning.'

'Yes, master,' Mother said meekly, and suddenly hugged him.

At their first door on the seventh floor nothing happened, nobody came. 'Still, there's _ _5_ _ inside,' Mother said. 'It's scary
here, I can feel it.' She pushed Barney back and dropped to her
_ _6_ _ and pulled up on the door. It didn't open at once and
when Barney started to kneel down to help her, she made him go
back. 'There's something strange here,' she whispered. 'I can feel
it, I feel shivery. It could be _ _7_ _ needing help, but I don't
know. I've got to see. I won't go in, I'll just look and call.' As she
said it she dropped down and pushed the tips of her fingers under
the door. This time it came open easily.

Inside the entrance hall there rose a rough sort of clothes tree
that _ _8_ _ to the ceiling. In the dimness Barney saw something
peel off the cross branches of the wooden tree. It flowed like
water down the main _ _9_ _ of the hall tree and slid towards the
door. It was a snake!

Barney leaped forward, pushed Mother aside and slammed the
door shut as the snake slithered towards her. Mother got up

_ 10 _ . She shook her head. 'The pets some people keep,' she whispered. But when she saw how scared Barney was she made a quick little _ 11 _ . 'Some keep rabbits, some keep snakes,' she said.

'Oh, he was big!' Barney said shakily. 'He was as thick around as I am! Big enough to crush all your ribs!' He felt his ribs. 'He must be a boa constrictor.'

'Oh, now, Barney,' Mother laughed, 'it wasn't a _ 12 _ . I saw it too. But it does mean we open no more doors, no matter what queer feelings I get.'

3 The White Horse Gang

by Nina Bawden

None of the local children would enter Gibbet Wood. It was a terrible place where you might be chased by a ghost or hung from a tree by the farmer. Abe, who lived on the other side of the wood invited Sam and Rose to visit him. They set out, with Sam trying to impress Rose with tales of his bravery.

It was a long way to the old mine workings on the other side of the Bent Hill, though it would not have been so far if they could have taken the short cut through Gibbet Wood. Sam explained why they could not do this, curdling his own blood with accounts of the Headless Hunter and the _ _1_ _ Farmer John.

'Course, Abe and I've been there lots of times, we went there Saturday as a matter of fact, but it wouldn't be safe for a girl.'

'I wouldn't be _ _2_ _ ,' Rose said.

'You mightn't think you would now, but you'd be scared all right.' Sam _ _3_ _ his voice to a hoarse whisper. 'The Headless Hunter rides through you like a cold wind, or he sits on his horse just a little way away, through the _ _4_ _ , and you think he's staring at you – it feels like he's staring at you – till you see he's got no head, only the stump of his neck with the blood all _ _5_ _ down it.'

'Ghosts can't kill you,' Rose said.

'They can drive you stark mad, _ _6_ _ . There's a boy over at Long Barrow who saw him one night and he went home with his face white and his eyes all staring and he's not spoken a word _ _7_ _ . He's ever so old now but his Mum has to look after him and feed him just as if he was a _ _8_ _ .' Sam smiled, pleased with this anecdote which he had invented on the spur of the moment.

'_ _9_ _ do you know he saw the Hunter, if he couldn't speak?' Rose asked.

'Oh. Well – he spoke *once*. When they found him – he ran home, you see, over the hill and he lost his shoes so that by the time he got back to his house his feet were all _ _10_ _ and bloody and he collapsed _ _11_ _ the door – *well*, when they found him, his mother picked him up and he cried out . . . .' Sam drew a _ _12_ _ breath – '. . . he cried out, "Oh Mother, the Hunter, the Hunter . . ." and after that he was sort of struck *dumb*. . . .'

Rose looked at him closely. 'I don't believe it,' she said. 'I don't believe in ghosts, anyway.'

4 A Dog So Small

by Philippa Pearce

Ben longed for a dog and his Grandfather promised he would have one for his birthday. However he was bitterly disappointed when his grandparents gave him a wool picture of the smallest dog in the world.

He put the little picture down on the seat beside him, leaned his head back, and closed his eyes, overwhelmed.

He had been staring at the woolwork dog, and now, with his _ _1_ _ shut, he still saw it, as if it were standing on the carriage-seat opposite. Such visions often appear against shut eyelids, when the open-eyed vision has been _ _2_ _ intent. Such visions quickly fade; but this did not. The image of the dog _ _3_ _ , exactly as in the picture: a pinky-fawn dog with pointed ears, and pop-eyed.

Only – only, the pinky-fawn was not done in wool, and the eye was not a jet bead. This dog was real. First of all, it just stood. Then it _ _4_ _ itself – first, its forelegs together; then, each hind leg with a separate stretch and shake. Then the dog turned its _ _5_ _ to look at Ben, so that Ben saw its other eye and the whole of the other side of its face, which the picture had never shown. But _ _6_ _ was not the picture of a dog; it was a _ _7_ _ dog – a particular dog.

'Chiquitito,' Ben said; and the dog cocked its head.

Ben had spoken _ _8_ _ . At the sound of his own voice, he opened his eyes in a fright. _ _9_ _ the dog had been standing, the young man sat looking at him in surprise; the _ _10_ _ businessman was also looking – and frowning. Ben felt himself blush. He forgot everything but the need not to seem _ _11_ _ , not to be noticed, questioned.

He turned to look out of the window. He kept his eyes wide open and blinked as briefly and infrequently as possible. He felt two _ 12 _ upon him.

After a while the young man spoke to him, offering to lend him one of his magazines. Ben devoted himself deeply to this, until the train was drawing into London.

5 Ballet Shoes

by Noel Streatfeild

About fifty years ago, three little orphan girls were adopted by a very unusual old man. He left them in the care of his great-niece and then went off on an expedition to collect fossils. As the years passed their money became short and several lodgers had to be taken in. One, who was a ballet teacher, managed to enrol Pauline, Petrova and Posy in the Children's Academy of Dancing and Stage Training.

Perhaps because they had been working so hard, Christmas day seemed the loveliest they had known. Nothing was very different from other Christmases; but somehow it seemed a particularly gay day. Their stockings bulged when they woke, and besides all the usual things in them, there were large white sugar pigs with pink noses and wool tails. When Nana came to tell them to get up, she had three parcels under her arm, and they, of course, had presents for her. Pauline had made her some handkerchiefs, and Petrova a needle-book full of needles, and Posy a blotter of two plaited paper mats stuck on cardboard. Nana had knitted _ _1_ _ of them a jumper with fluffy rabbit's wool round the cuffs and collars. Pauline's was blue, Petrova's orange, and Posy's pink. They _ _2_ _ put them on for breakfast. On the breakfast table were chocolates for them from Theo; everybody else's presents were waiting for the Christmas tree after tea. They went to church – even Posy – and sang 'Hark, the Herald Angels', 'Oh Come, all Ye Faithful', and 'The First Noël'. They had been afraid that perhaps they would only get one that they knew and the rest some _ _3_ _ tune that was supposed to belong to Christmas and did not really. The turkey and plum pudding and crystallized fruits and things they had for lunch, as Posy was not

_ _4_ _ to sit up to dinner. After lunch Sylvia read to them while they did an _ _5_ _ jigsaw that she had got especially for Christmas afternoon. Then there was tea, and Cook had made a most _ _6_ _ cake with a Father Christmas and reindeer on it, and as well, three large gold stars which she said was what she hoped the children would be.

It was when they went into Doctor Smith's room for the Christmas tree they had the big _ _7_ _ of the day. Sylvia always had a Christmas tree for them; but this was not like any tree they had seen before. It was the usual fir tree; but every branch was covered with glittering frost, which made the tree look as though it were magic.

After the last present had been opened and the last candle on the tree blown out, they played charades and hide-and-seek all _ _8_ _ the house. It was great fun; but everybody suddenly thought about the _ _9_ _ . This was the end, and Christmas day was over for another year, which was a miserable feeling. _ 10_ _ Cook and Clara went away to get dressed for their own Christmas party downstairs, and then Nana took Posy to bed. After that, _ 11_ _ they had supper of cold turkey and meringues, the day was terribly finished, and both Pauline and Petrova felt as though they had been balloons, but were now _ 12_ _ and had gone flat.

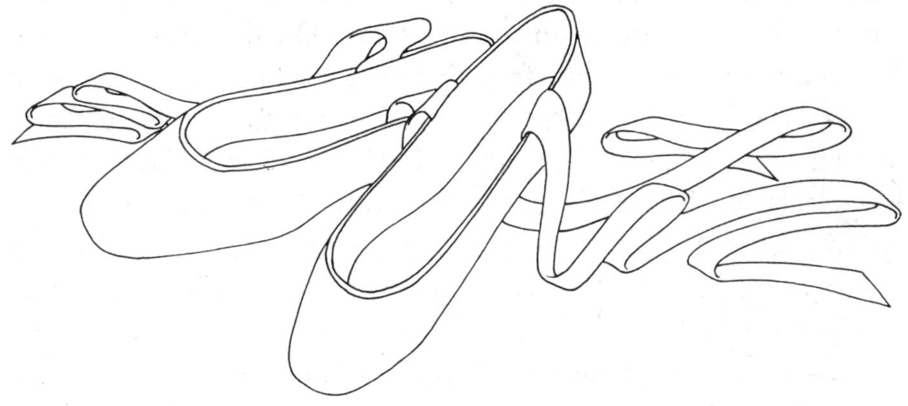

6 Hurricane

by Andrew Salkey

In Jamaica, where Joe and his family live, the weather is very different from here. When the Meteorological Office warned of an approaching hurricane everyone had to nail wood over their windows and secure their doors and anything else that might move. After that all they could do was to take shelter, listen to the radio and wait.

As I sat down beside Mama on the sofa, I was just in time to hear the announcer say: 'We have only just received the following progress-reports from amateur radio-, telegraph-, and certain private telephone-messages, coming in from all over Kingston and Saint Andrew . . .'

While the announcer was talking, I imagined I saw the extent of the _ _1_ _ done to places like the Ward Theatre and the open-air cinemas like the Rialto, the Palace, and the Gaiety. The Ward must have been so _ _2_ _ smashed that I was sure it would look like an old ruin. After all, it's not a modern building, _ _3_ _ the oldest theatre I've ever seen, and not all that strong enough to stand up to the battering of a hurricane.

The wooden seats in the open-air cinemas must have been soaked through and, for all I knew, wrenched from the concrete flooring. And all the reels of film and _ _4_ _ must have been completely ruined by now.

'Can you _ _5_ _ what's happened to the Straw Market at Victoria Pier?' Mama said.

'Blown _ _6_ _ , I'd say,' Papa told her. 'Sheds and _ _7_ _ .' He shook his head and continued, 'Of course, the thing that's really _ _8_ _ will be the damage done to the Corporation's drinking-water reservoirs, and to the light and power stations.'

We listened again to the radio announcer. He was saying: '. . . and the roofs of a number of dwelling houses have been either partially or wholly _ _9_ _ off. It has been reported that exposed vehicles are being washed away, and in some places damaged by _ 10 _ wind-blown objects. It has also been reported that lightning has struck trees and out-buildings in the City and on _ 11 _ on the North Coast and on the mid-southern side and eastern tip of the island. It has been estimated that Kingston has never, within living memory, experienced . . .'

'All the broken telegraph-poles, smashed trees,' Papa was talking again, 'and the flying _ 12 _ from the wind-shields of parked cars, and that sort of thing.'

I immediately thought about the force of the wind and the lashing of the rain outside. They both sounded extraordinarily louder than ever before, especially after what Papa had just said.

7 The Town that Went South

by Clive King

Gargoyle, the cat, was the first one to discover that, during a stormy night, the whole town of Ramsly had come adrift from the rest of Britain and was floating South. It stopped for a few days on reaching France but when the next storm began – off they all floated again. The missing words are all ADJECTIVES.

There were two terrible days and nights of storm at sea. There was a time when the whole town really did take on a heaving, pitching motion, the church bells rang themselves and, in the houses, those most homely and secure things, the mantelpieces over the hearths, were no longer _ _1_ _ places to keep porcelain vases or souvenirs of Margate. But when the storm had done its worst, the old houses of Ramsly were still standing and only a few rather _ _2_ _ little new sheds by the Strand had been carried away. And the floating town came out into a region of warm breezes, blue sky and _ _3_ _ clear water, and settled down into its new life as if in a dream.

Anyone could tell that the town was moving South. The creepers that used to struggle a _ _4_ _ inches a year up the old _ _5_ _ walls of Watchbell Street began to spread over the eaves and clamber up the chimneys, and the air was full of their scent. The prickly pear that _ _6_ _ Mrs Cosset had kept for years in a pot on her window-sill was knocked into the back yard one day and smashed into pieces, and every _ _7_ _ piece took root in the cobbles so that before long she had a job to get to her dustbin. Gargoyle, and the old men who sat in the sun whenever they could, found to their surprise that they were now choosing the shade instead.

One day Miss Holly of Ye Olde Oake Beame Café was seen putting her tables and chairs out on the pavement and, though people were a bit shocked at first, they soon got used to the idea and would sit for hours under the awning over their cups of tea. _ _8_ _ things than that happened. More and more people were suspected of spending the afternoons in, or rather on, their beds. The Old Wives' Guild were particularly upset about the possibility of some of their members getting this _ _9_ _ habit, and organized daily knitting and sewing parties to keep themselves busy during the _ 10 _ afternoons. They were even more upset when old Mrs Guffle, one of their _ 11 _ members, suddenly exclaimed half-way through a _ 12 _ sleepy meeting: 'I don't know why we want to waste our time making *more* clothes, I'm sure. I'm going home to take a few things off.'

8 Autumn Term

by Antonia Forest

As a pupil, in her first term at Kingscote Boarding School, Nicola was not doing too well. After getting into various unintentional scrapes she decided to slip away from school, on her free afternoon, to visit her brother, Giles, who was in the Navy. His ship had docked at Port Wade a few miles away from the school and Nicola had no trouble in disguising her uniform and then travelling to Port Wade by train. Once there it was only a short walk to the docks.
The missing words are all ADVERBS.

She strolled easily, her hands in her pockets, pausing every now and then to stare fascinated at some small cargo ship alongside, her hold and decks crammed with coal or timber. She loitered past, grinning shyly at the fair, friendly sailors who smiled back and shouted to one another in tongues she could not begin to understand. Tim might have known . . . Nicola dismissed Tim impatiently, avoiding the sprawled legs of some boys about her own age who hung over the quay-side fishing for dabs, but _ _1_ _ catching only small crabs whose legs moved _ _2_ _ as they were drawn up, to be detached from the hook and dropped into the sea _ _3_ _ .

A church clock chimed _ _4_ _ from the town – a three-quarter chime, not specially helpful until the hour struck. Nicola, jerked back into time once more, began to hurry, and bumped into a sailor carrying a kit-bag. The air had begun to smell _ _5_ _ of oil, and she recollected, with a sense of shock, that she was supposed to be looking for Giles. She hoped, with a faint touch of uneasiness, that she hadn't _ _6_ _ passed him.

She glanced over her shoulder. She seemed to have come a very

long way. Almost without realizing it, she had come into the midst
of the crane and derrick area she had seen from the first quay. The
quays were very crowded here; she would have to go pretty _ _7_ _
so as not to miss Giles . . .

Suddenly she was out of the crowded quarter and at the end of
the docks. The quay-side stretched before her, quiet, _ _8_ _ de-
serted, with damp paper blowing over the cement blocks and dark
flat water slapping against the wall. She walked on _ _9_ _ and
stood at the very end, gazing over the long stretch of water which
lay between the quay-side and the dark, cloud-topped downs
beyond. Nearer to the downs than to the quay the three destroyers
lay _ 10 _ in a patch of pale sunshine which struck them from
between the hurrying clouds and then raced on across the water.

So that was that. Giles was _ 11 _ on board and she wouldn't
see him. She felt flat and disappointed, the pictured pleasures of the
afternoon thinning into nothingness like smoke in a high wind.
There seemed nothing more to do except walk back along the
quays, return to the station and wait for the next train. She hadn't
even enough with her to give herself tea . . . Nicola, peering into
her purse to make certain that she really did possess only three-
pence ha'penny, gasped _ 12 _ as though a cold wave had dren-
ched her and fumbled in her pocket in wild agitation. But it was
true. Of course it was true. She had only bought a single ticket.
And now she would never be able to return. Never.

9 Lottie and Lisa

by Erich Kästner

Lottie came from Germany and Lisa came from Austria. They met quite by chance at a children's summer holiday camp. They were identical and soon realised they were twins. Lottie was quiet, well behaved and a good cook who lived with their mother. Lisa was boisterous and high spirited and lived with their father. After filling notebooks full of information about each other's lives they changed places to meet their other parent but it was not as easy as it had seemed.

Lisa was cooking. She had put on one of Mummy's aprons, and was spinning to and fro like a top between the gas-cooker, where the saucepans were boiling over the gas-jets, and the table on which lay the open cookery-book. Every few minutes she lifted a saucepan-lid. When the boiling water hissed and boiled over, she jumped. How much salt should she put in the noodles? 'Half a teaspoonful!' How much celery salt? 'A pinch!' How much, for goodness' sake, is a pinch? And then, 'Grate a nutmeg.' Where were the nutmegs? Where was the grater?

She _ _1_ _ in drawers, climbed on chairs, looked into all the canisters, glanced at the clock on the wall. She jumped down from a chair, grabbed a fork, lifted a lid, burned her fingers, squealed, stabbed the beef with the _ _2_ _ – No, it wasn't done yet.

She stood stock still, holding the fork in her hand. What was she looking for? Oh yes, the nutmeg and grater. Goodness! What was that _ _3_ _ so harmlessly beside the cookery-book? – The mixed herbs. They had to be cleaned and put in the broth! Down with the fork, up with the knife. Was the meat _ _4_ _ yet? And where were the gratemeg and the nutter? Oh dear, the grater and the nutmeg? The mixed herbs had _ _5_ _ to be washed under the tap, and the carrots had to be scraped. Ah-uh! You had to watch out that you didn't cut yourself! And when the meat was done you had to take _ _6_ _ out of the saucepan and drain off the bones. For that you needed a colander. And Mummy would be here in half an hour! And twenty minutes _ _7_ _ she arrived you had to drop the noodles in boiling water. What a mess the kitchen was _ _8_ _ . And the nutmeg! And the colander! And the grater! And . . . and . . . and . . .

Lisa flopped down on the kitchen chair. Oh Lottie! It's not so easy being your own sister!

The clock ticked on.

In twenty-nine minutes Mummy would be here! . . . In twenty-eight and a half minutes! . . . In twenty-eight minutes! . . . In twenty-seven and a half minutes!

Lisa clenched her fists with _ _9_ _ and got up to start again. As she did so, she growled to herself. 'If I can't manage this –'

But that's the _ 10 _ thing about cooking. Determination is all very well if you want to jump off a tower. But will-power is not enough when it comes to cooking beef and noodles.

And when Mrs Horn came home, tired with the day's exertions, she did not find a smiling _ 11 _ housekeeper awaiting her. Not at all. She found a completely _ 12 _ scrap of misery, a slightly damaged, confused, crumpled little object, from whose mouth, twisted ready for tears, came the words, 'Mummy, don't be angry! I think I've unlearnt cooking.'

10 Peter Pan

by J. M. Barrie

After a fight with Captain Hook, Peter Pan was left on Marooner's Rock in the middle of the Mermaid's Lagoon. The water was rising fast and Peter was too weak to either fly or swim away.

Steadily the waters rose till they were nibbling at his feet; and to pass the time until they made their final gulp, he watched the only thing moving on the lagoon. He thought it was a piece of floating paper, perhaps part of the kite, and wondered idly how long it would take to drift ashore.

_ _1_ _ he noticed as an odd thing that it was undoubtedly out upon the lagoon with some definite purpose, for it was fighting the tide, and sometimes winning; and when it won, Peter, always sympathetic to the weaker side, could not help clapping; it was such a gallant piece of paper.

It was not really a piece of paper; it was the Never bird, making _ _2_ _ efforts to reach Peter on her nest. By working her wings, in a way she had learned since the nest fell into the water, she was able to some extent to guide her strange craft, but by the time Peter recognized her she was _ _3_ _ exhausted. She had come to save him, to give him her nest, though there were eggs in it. I rather wonder at the bird, for though he had been nice to her, he had also sometimes _ _4_ _ her.

She called out to him what she had come for, and he called out to her what was she doing there; but of course neither of them understood the other's _ _5_ _ .

Nevertheless the bird was determined to save him if she could, and _ _6_ _ one last mighty effort she propelled the nest against the rock. Then up she flew; deserting her eggs, so as to make her meaning clear.

I forget _ _7_ _ I have told you that there was a stave on the rock, driven into it by some buccaneers of long ago to mark the site of _ _8_ _ treasure. The children had discovered the glittering hoard, and when in _ _9_ _ mood used to fling showers of moidores, diamonds, pearls and pieces of eight to the gulls, who _ 10 _ upon them for food, and then flew away, raging at the scurvy trick that had been played upon them. The stave was still there, and on it Starkey had hung his hat, a deep tarpaulin, watertight, with a broad brim. Peter put the eggs into this hat and set it on the _ 11 _ . It floated beautifully.

The Never bird saw at once what he was up to, and screamed her admiration of him; and, alas, Peter crowed his agreement with her. Then he got into the nest, reared the stave in it as a mast, and hung up his shirt for a sail. At the same moment the bird fluttered down upon the hat and once more sat _ 12 _ on her eggs. She drifted in one direction, and he was borne off in another, both cheering.

11 The Children of Green Knowe

by Lucy Boston

Many years ago, when there had been flooding all around Green Knowe, Linnet was very ill. The only person who could go for the doctor was Toby, Linnet's brother. His mother told him to go the shortest way over the wooden bridge and up the hill.

Toby pulled on his long, loose-topped boots and took his thick cloak and ran down to the stables. He saddled Feste, and as he put on the bridle he talked to him, saying, 'Feste, we must get the doctor for Linnet.'

The horse, who had lowered his head to receive the bridle, nuzzled Toby's cheek and understood very well that he was troubled. He gave a little neigh, and as soon as Toby's leg was over the saddle he whisked round and started off. It was not dark yet, the sky was dim green like water, and shallow water was over the roads. As they _ _1_ _ off the mud flew up like a dirty fountain round them. The lane took them for four miles and ended at the wooden bridge. The river looked very nasty in the half light. The current _ _2_ _ and pushed and the middle of the river seemed higher than the sides, as if it had been squashed up. The bridge was still well above the water.

Toby _ _3_ _ his horse to a walking pace lest the wood should be slippery, and expected that Feste would cross it as he had done hundreds of times before. But no; Feste, the obedient, would not cross it. He _ _4_ _ and waltzed but he would not go on. Toby talked to him, coaxed him, scolded him, pulling his head round to face the bridge again and again, but all in vain. At last, for the first time in his life he _ _5_ _ his switch and lashed him. Feste reared up and struck at the air with outstretched fore-feet so that it was all

Toby could do to hang on in the saddle. When in this way Feste
had exhibited his height and his strength and his angry pride, he
came down from his prancing and without warning leapt the high
hedge at the side of the lane. He _ _6_ _ down the bank with his
forefeet stuck out before him, and after sidling some distance along
the river bank he trumpeted a challenging neigh and, plunging
into the cold ugly river, began to swim.

Toby could feel the powerful water buffeting and _ _7_ _ his leg
on the upstream side, dragging and snatching at it on the other. It
was as though the river were determined to separate him from
Feste. Now and then a branch would hit him as a broken tree went
past. Once they were tangled up in some floating straw from a rick.
It nearly _ _8_ _ Toby out of the saddle, but he just managed to
push it away. As they swam, they were swept gradually down-
stream towards the bridge. Toby, crouched over Feste's labouring
shoulders, could feel that he was striking out for his life. His ears
were straining forward and his eyes too, so that Toby could see the
whites, and he snorted and grunted with his muzzle just above the
water.

They reached the farther bank only a few yards upstream from
the bridge, and _ _9_ _ up on the other side, Feste digging in with
his toes while he gathered his hocks for the last great effort. At the
top of the bank he stood with heaving sides and trembling shoulders shaking his heavy wet mane and hanging his head.

'Feste, you mad, crazy horse! Whatever possessed you to do
that?' _ 10 _ Toby, twisting in the saddle to pull off his loose
boots one by one to empty the water out of them. He was soaked to
the neck and bitterly cold. His teeth _ 11 _ and his hands were
blue. 'Stand, Feste, stand, you madman! The devil's in you!'

Feste was backing away from the bridge and flinging his head up
and down so that Toby had to give up trying to wring water out of

his cloak.

Suddenly there came a hair-raising scream, the scream of rend-ing wood, sounding almost like an animal in panic. The wooden bridge twisted and _ 12 _ under his eyes and, with cracks like cannon fire, collapsed and was swept in a tangled mass down-stream. Feste screamed too, and they were off together at full gallop up the hill in the fading light.

12 Grinny

by Nicholas Fisk

When Great Aunt Emma (GAE for short) suddenly arrived at Tim and Beth's house she was a complete stranger to them. They had never even known their grandmother had a sister but their parents welcomed her and let her stay, even though she behaved in a very strange manner. On one occasion when she slipped on ice and Beth ran to help her Beth became very frightened. Tim had to persuade Beth to tell him exactly what happened. This is how he wrote it in his diary.

So I made her tell me just what it was she saw. She started off by repeating that I would never believe her and so on, but in the end it came down to this – I am choosing my words very carefully so as not to distort what she said –

'She was lying on the ground in a heap. She was not groaning or moaning, just lying there and kicking her _ _1_ _ , trying to get up. I went close to her and got hold of her _ _2_ _ so that I could help pull her up. She did not say anything to me, like "Help me" or "My wrist hurts" – she just tried to get up. When I seized her elbows, I saw her wrist. The hand was dangling. The wrist was so badly broken that the skin was all cut open in a gash and the bones were _ _3_ _ .'

I told Beth I understood all this, but she seemed unwilling to go on. She looked at me and wailed, 'Oh, it's no good, you'll never believe me!' but I made her go on. She said:

'The skin was gashed open but there was no blood. The bones stuck out but they were not made of _ _4_ _ bone – they were made of shiny steel!'

I have these words right. Beth did say what I have written. I am quite certain about asking her what sort of bones, what sort of steel and so on. Her answers were, that the steel was _ _5_ _ shiny and that the bones looked smaller than proper bones – more like umbrella ribs. When I asked her what umbrella ribs look like, she answered (correctly) that they are made of channels of steel, _ _6_ _ solid rods like knitting needles. She said that GAE's bones were in 'little collections' of these steel ribs and that the skin had been _ _7_ _ by a few of the ribs breaking away from a main cluster and coming through the skin.

So I asked her again about the absence of blood and she was _ _8_ _ . She said there was no blood, no blood at all, the skin was just split _ _9_ _ . I asked her what colour the skin was and she said the same colour outside as in. I said, well, there must have been meaty stuff where the bones were, but she said no. There was _ _10_ _ but the steel ribs and that the skin was just a _ _11_ _ layer 'like the fat on a mutton chop before it is cooked', but with a tear in it.

As I was thinking of all the things that might have caused Beth to think she saw what she said she saw she began again. 'I saw her wrist mend! I saw it heal _ _12_ _ !' she said.

I must say, this gave me goosepimples. I said, 'What do you mean?' and Beth told me that as she watched, *the skin came together over the broken bones leaving a bump covering the breaks.* That was when Beth became really frightened and ran inside.